THE CHARACTER OF A COMPLETE EVANGELICAL PASTOR

Drawn by Christ (Matt. 24:45-47)

JOHN FLAVEL

EDITED BY DANIEL BARDEN

The Character of a Complete Evangelical Pastor

By John Flavel

Edited by Daniel Barden

Cover design: Cassie Parsley

INTRODUCTION

John Flavel (1627-1691) was a Presbyterian minister in the town of Dartmouth, Devon. Being the son of a pastor, Flavel entered the ministry after his time at University College, Oxford. It was at Oxford that Flavel finally came to saving faith in Christ. After his conversion, Flavel eventually took up a pastorate in Dartmouth after the awful tragedy of losing his wife. Dartmouth was a town known for its fishing and harbour, and was a relatively wealthy part of England. It was here that Flavel spent 35 years ministering to Christ's sheep and preaching the gospel. But it wasn't all plain sailing for the beloved Puritan. Flavel was one of many Puritans ejected from their pulpits in 1662 due to the Act of Uniformity which sought to stamp out Puritanism in England. Flavel was banned from entering Dartmouth, and could no longer minister to the sheep he had given his life to. But rumour has it that such was the heart of Flavel for his people, that he continued to enter the town disguised, in order to pastor to the needs of the sheep. In 1671, the ban was reversed, and Flavel returned to Dartmouth and received a fruitful ministry from the Lord. Flavel spent much of his time writing, and many of his sermons were put to paper. His famous collection of sermons on the person and work of Christ (The Fountain of Life) have been profoundly beneficial to believers throughout the centuries. Flavel also wrote a book on the Mystery of Providence, which is probably his most famous, and most popular work.

But tucked away at the back of the 6th volume of Flavel's works is a hidden gem titled, "The character of a complete evangelical pastor." This is the book that you are holding in your hands. It is here that Flavel instructs ministers in their most important work. It is my prayer that this small book will encourage and spur you on with the great work of ministry. The work is lightly edited, with some added headings to make it easier to read.

THE CHARACTER OF A COMPLETE EVANGELICAL PASTOR

Who then is a faithful and wise servant whom the Lord hath made ruler over his house, to give them meat in due season? Blessed is that servant, whom his Lord, when he cometh, shall find so doing. Verily, I say unto you, that he shall make him ruler over all his goods (Matthew. 24:45-47).

This great and solemn assembly, (met upon a greater and more solemn account,) brings to my mind those words, and with the words, a very sensible touch of the same affection, with which the church uttered them, 'Children, which thou shalt have after thou hast lost the other, shall say again in thine ears, The place is too strait for me: Give place to me, that I may dwell. Then shalt thou say in thine heart. Who hath begotten me these, seeing I have lost my children, and I am desolate; a captive, and removing to and fro? And who hath brought up these? Behold, I was left alone: these, where had they been? - Isa. 49:20-21. Words, big with holy admiration and wonder, at her strange and sudden increase and multiplication, after such a wasting time as these seventy sad years had been to her. This was a miraculous and surprizing work of God, in their eyes. We have had our wasting time, as well as they; multitudes of faithful and prudent ministers have been swept into their graves by ejections, banishments, imprisonments, and heart-breaking silencing's. Whence then are all these which our eyes behold this day! Who hath begotten us, and brought up these? These, where had they been; and out of what secret recesses are they come? Many thought the days of our prosperity, and opportunities of our service, had been numbered and finished, and that God had no more work (except suffering work) for us; when lo, above and beyond the desponding thoughts, and unbelieving fears of our hearts, we are here this day in a numerous assembly, with peace and liberty, to consult the affairs of Christs kingdom. Yea, to the joy of our souls, we see the plummets and lines, once more in the hands of our Zerubbabels; Zech. 4:10. Who hath despised the day of small things? For they shall rejoice, and shall see the plummet in the hand of Zerubbabel, with those seven; they are the eyes of the Lord, which run to and fro through the whole earth.' Our prudent repairers, co-working with the divine providence, expressed emblematically by the seven eyes, will bring weak and contemptible beginnings, to happy and blessed results and issues. What shall one now answer the messengers of the churches? That God hath founded Zion; and the power of his people shall trust in it. We are met this day in all hearty loyalty to the government, and peaceableness to the national church-establishment, to review and consider the cases of our respective congregations; which I doubt we shall find too like that description, Prov. 24:31 "all over-grown with thorns and nettles, and the stone-wall broke down." Thus ignorance and error have overspread the people, and the wall of discipline greatly decayed. Our business is to cleanse our churches, and repair their walls; that so they may become gardens of delight, and beds of spices, for Christ to walk and take pleasure in. You have ordered this meeting to be opened with a sermon, and demanded that work to my hand, by your earnest and unanimous call. I wish the work may not suffer by your choice. When I considered the quality and occasion of this assembly, my thoughts quickly centred themselves in those words of our Lord, which I have read unto you: ' Who then is a faithful and wise servant, whom his Lord hath made ruler over his household, to give them meat in due season?' &c. Here we find ourselves in a parable. A parable is the veil of some divine truth: whilst we are embodied and veiled with flesh, truth must embody and veil herself too, in order to our freer converses with it. There is much truth and reason in that observation of the ancient cabbalists: " The supreme light never descends without a covering." Yea, saith Dionysius, the supposed Areopagate, " It is impossible that a divine beam should otherwise shine to us, except it be covered with variety of sacred veils, and umbrages." Not to spend much time about the order and relation of the text; Christ had been solemnly warning the disciples, and all the Christian world, of his most certain (though secret) coming to judgment; and therefore to beware of luxury, idleness, and security, the sins of the world ; and that all be found at his coming, watchful and diligent in their proper places of duty. This exhortation he infers, from what common prudence would teach any servant, especially any steward of an house to do, to whom his Lord hath committed the care of his family. It is agreed by all, that the words have a special and immediate respect to gospel-ministers, the stewards of Christ's house, or church, to whom Christ, the Lord of the family, hath trusted the care and dispensation of the affairs thereof.

And in them we find, I. An evangelical pastor described. II. The reward of such as answer that description, propounded.

1. A description of an Evangelical Pastor

Christ's description of an evangelical pastor, ver. 45. which he doth by two excellent and essential properties, or qualifications, faithful and wise; both which make up the character of a complete gospel-minister: for if he be faithful, he deceives not others; and if wise, or prudent, he is not apt to be deceived himself: his prudence suffers not deceivers easily to impose upon him; and his faithfulness will not suffer him knowingly to impose upon his people. His prudence will enable him to discern, and his faithfulness oblige him to distribute wholesome food to his flock.

These two therefore meeting together, make a pastor after God's own heart, according to Jer. 3:15. Both these are found in an interrogative form of speech in the text, but it is agreed, that 'Tis' is put conditionally for 'ei tis' and is rather hypothetical, than interrogatory: but in this form of speech it insinuates the rarity and difficulty of finding such a servant. And Chrysostom, by way of admiration, 'How rare and excellent would such servants be?' These are their properties,

2. The Pastor's reward

The reward of those that answer these characters, is propounded, 1. In proper, 2. In metaphorical terms.

1. In proper terms; Blessed is that servant, ver. 46. he is certainly blessed of God, whatever his usage be from men. If he be faithful, all his prudence will not secure him from the hatred and persecution of men, but it is enough that Christ calls and counts him blessed; and those whom he blesseth, are truly and eternally blessed.

2. In metaphorical terms; ver. 47. "Verily, I say unto you, that he shall make him ruler over all his goods."" In allusion to the custom of great kings and generals, who use to prefer and advance discreet and faithful servants to places of eminent trust, profit, and honour; as Daniel and Joseph were. The sense thus cleared, runs naturally and easily into this,

THE DOCTRINE

That our Lord Jesus Christ will amply reward the faithful and prudent stewards of his house, in the day of their account.

This point will open itself to you in these three doctrinal branches.

1. That ministers, in a special sense, are the stewards of Christ' house.

2. Faithfulness and prudence are necessary qualifications of Christ's stewards.

3. Wherever these are found, Christ will abundantly reward them.

1. Minister's, in a special sense, are the stewards, or chief servants of Christ's house. So speaks the apostle, 1 Cor. 4:1. "Let a man account of us as the ministers of Christ, and stewards of the mysteries of God." To them he hath committed the dispensation of the word and sacraments, which contain the great mysteries of the kingdom of God. Every private person, who hath received any talent from God, (and to be sure the meanest among us hath one talent at least,) is a steward, and will be called to an account for the employment, or non-employment of that talent in the audit-day. But ministers are stewards in the strict and special sense: Christ distinguishes them from the others, as porters from the rest of the servants, Mark 13:84. Nor may any assume that office, but by order from Christ the Master of the family. But this is too obvious to stay longer upon it.

2. We will therefore immediately take into consideration, the properties or qualification of the stewards of Christ: which are, 1. Faithfulness. 2. Prudence. And consider them, 1. Distinctly. 2. Conjunctly.

FAITHFULNESS

1. Faithfulness is an essential requisite to a steward, 1 Cor. 4:2. It is required in stewards, that a man be found faithful. What ground is there for trust, where there is no truth? Hence is that solemn charge, 2 Tim. 2:2, to commit that great trust of the ministry to faithful men. And Paul blesseth God, 1 Tim. 1:11-12 who had accounted him faithful, and put him into the ministry. This faithful, as it respects to God, ourselves, and the flocks committed to us, includes,

1. Pure and spiritual aims and intentions.

2. Sincerity and integrity of heart.

3. Diligence in the discharge of duty.

4. Impartiality in the administration of Christ's house.

5. And unshaken constancy and perseverance to the end.

1. Spiritual aims

Ministerial faithfulness includes pure and spiritual aims and intentions for God. A servant is not his own, but his master's honour, and interest, he must design and aim at. Fidelity will not endure self-ends, disguised with a pretence of zeal for Christ. It is said of the master workmen of the temple, 2 Kings 22:7, that there was no reckoning made with them of the money collected for that use, because they dealt faithfully, i.e. they had given sufficient proof that they appropriated not a farthing to themselves, but truly applied it to the public, sacred end and use, to which it was given. O let us be all such faithful master-builders of the house of our God! Let us say, not our interest, but Christ's, not our glory, but his. Pure ends in our service, will give abundant comfort at the end of our service, a care, brethren, of all artifices and designs to accommodate carnal interests, under a shew of devotion to God. Timothy is our pattern in this, of whom Paul saith, Phil. 2:20-21, 'I have no man like minded, who will naturally care for your state; for all seek their own, not the things that are Jesus Christ's." Where the word naturally is not opposed to spiritually, but to artificially. Others had the art to cloak self-ends under Christ's honour; but Timothy was ignorant of such unfaithful tricks and artifices.

2. Sincerity

Ministerial faithfulness imports personal sincerity. So the word signifies, where it is said of Abraham, that God found his heart faithful; that is, sincere before him. (Neh. 9:8.) A faithful minister is a sincere-hearted minister. And herein, brethren, O herein, or in nothing, let us approve ourselves the ministers of Christ: Let this be our "rejoicing, that in all sincerity, and godly simplicity, we have had our conversations in this world," 2 Cor. 1:12. And the rather let us be careful in this, because no sin is more apt to insinuate itself into our hearts, and duties, than hypocrisy. We, of all men, are most in danger to be deceived by it: For our employment lying in, and about spiritual things, we are, on that account, stiled spiritual men, Hos. 9:7. But it is plain, from that very place, that a man may be objectively a spiritual, and all the while subjectively a carnal man. Believe it, brethren, it is easier to declaim, like an orator, against a thousand, sins of others, than it is to mortify one sin, like Christians, in ourselves; to be more industrious in our pulpits, than in our closets; to preach twenty sermons to our people, than one to our own hearts. Believe it, sirs, all our reading, studying, and preaching, is but trifling hypocrisy, till the things read, studied, and preached, be felt in some degree upon our own hearts. We tell our people (the Lord help us to tell the same to our own hearts) that there are similar, as well as saving works of the Spirit, by which their (and why not our own) souls may be lost?

3. Diligence

Ministerial faithfulness includes ministerial diligence. A slothful servant cannot be a faithful servant. Matt. 25:21 "His Lord said unto him, Well done, thou good and faithful servant," &c. And ver. 26. " His Lord answered, and said unto him. Thou wicked and slothful servant, &:c. I may say to him that snatched at the ministry, as Henry IV. did to his son, that hastily snatched at the crown, He little knows what a heap of cares and toils he snatched at. 'The labourers of the ministry will exhaust the very marrow from your bones, hasten old age and death.' They are fitly compared to the toil of men in harvest, to the labours of a woman in travail, and to the agonies of soldiers in the extremity of a battle. We must watch when others sleep. And indeed it is not so much the expense of our labours, as the loss of them, that kills us. It is not with us, as with other labourers: They find their work as they leave it, so do not we. Sin and Satan unravel almost all we do, the impressions we make on our people's souls in one sermon, vanish before the next. How many truths have we to study! How many wiles of Satan, and mysteries of corruption, to detect! How many cases of conscience to resolve! Yea, we must fight in defence of the truths we preach, as well as study them to paleness, and preach them unto faintness: but well-spent head, heart, lungs, and all; welcome pained breasts, aching backs, and trembling legs; if we can by all but approve ourselves Christ's faithful servants, and hear that joyful voice from his mouth, 'Well done, good and faithful servants.'

4. Impartiality

Ministerial faithfulness includes our impartiality in all the administrations of Christ's house. He that is partial, cannot be faithful. O with what extraordinary solemnity doth Paul set on this exhortation upon Timothy! 'I charge thee before God, and the Lord Jesus Christ, and the elect angels, that thou observe these things, without preferring one before another, doing nothing by partiality,' 1 Tim. 5:21. Brethren, you will shortly appear before an impartial God, see that ye be impartial stewards; take the same care, manifest the same love, attend with the same diligence, the poorest and weakest souls that are committed to your care, as you do the rich, the great, and honourable. Remember all souls are rated at one value in your Master's book, and your Redeemer paid as much for the one as for the other. Civil differences must be civilly acknowledged, but these have no place in our spiritual administrations.

5. Steadfastness

Lastly, Ministerial faithfulness includes constancy and steadfastness: Not a backsliding, or flinching servant. Rev. 2:10. 'Be thou faithful, (i. e. fixed and constant) to the death, and I will give thee a crown of life.' We look for happiness, as long as God is in heaven; and he expects constancy, as long as we are on earth. Many of us have cause to bless the Lord, and greatly to rejoice in his goodness this day, who enabled us to be steadfast and unmoveable in the trials that have passed over us; and when the great earthquake shaked down our liberties, our estates, and made our hearts to shake, yet our resolutions for God and his truth, stood firm and unshaken: Our hearts turned not back, nor did our steps decline, though we were broken in the place of dragons, and covered with the shadow of death. This we wholly owe to him that holds the stars in his right-hand, but our warfare is not yet ended. Our faithfulness is not yet faithfulness to the death; we hope it will shortly be called so, whilst it thus involves our self-denial, sincerity, diligence, impartiality, and constancy. These are the principal things included in the first qualification of ministerial faithfulness. In the next place let us weigh and value,

PRUDENCE

The second qualification in the text, viz. ministerial prudence. The Lord's servant must not only be faithful; but prudent, discreet, and wise. Fidelity and honesty make a good

Christian; but the addition of prudence to fidelity, makes a good steward. Faithfulness will fix the eye upon the right end; but it is prudence must direct to the proper means of attaining it. If we look into Rev. 4:6, 7, we shall there find a stately emblem of true gospel ministers. They are men full of eyes. They have eyes looking before them to God for direction, behind them to the flocks they lead, and within them to their own hearts; lest after they have preached to others, themselves become cast-aways. They have also six wings; with two they cover their faces, manifesting their deep reverence of God; with two their feet, manifesting the humble sense of their infirmities; and with two they fly with cheerful expedition in the service of God. They have not only the courage of the lion, the strength of the ox, the loftiness of the eagle, but the face of a man, i.e. prudence and discretion. The use of prudence to a minister of Christ is unspeakably great; It not only gives clearness and perspicacity to the mind, by freeing it from passions and corporeal impressions, enabling it thereby to apprehend what is best to be done; but enables it in its deliberations, about the means, to make choice of the most apt and proper; and directs the application of them in the fittest season, without precipitation, by too much haste; or hazard, by too tedious delay. And judge you, brethren, by this, what an interest the affairs of Christ's kingdom have in this second qualification. I know there is a carnal policy, an unworthy pusillanimity, that often shrewd themselves under the name of prudence; I have nothing to do with mock graces here: My business is to shew you, in what particulars true ministerial prudence is highly serviceable to the affairs of Christ's house, or kingdom. And this I will briefly discourse in two respects.

The eye of prudence must look,

1. To our own personal work, to see that be well done.

2. To others who work,

(1). With us as friends, that we may have assistance from them.

(2). Or against us as enemies, that our work be not ruined by them.

PRUDENCE IN PERSONAL WORK

1. Prudence will direct the servants of Christ, in their own proper ministerial work, that it be well done. And in order thereto, it will guide them in their deliberations to the six following proper means, and excellent expedients.

1. Catechising

Prudence will direct us, to lay a good foundation of knowledge in our people's souls, by catechising and instructing them in the principles of Christianity, without which we labour in vain. Except you have a knowing people, you are not like to have a gracious people. St. Paul's prudentials lay much in this, 1 Cor. 3:10. As a wise master-builder, I have laid the foundation. And indeed this is the master-piece of a master-builder. All your excellent sermons will be dashed to pieces, upon the rock of your people's ignorance. You can never pitch upon a better project, to promote and secure the success of your labours, than catechizing. What age of Christianity ever produced more lively and steadfast Christians, than the first ages? And then the care of this duty most eminently flourished in the churches. Clemens

Alexandrianus, Origen, Optatus, Basil, Austin, and Ambrose, were all catechists: And it is the opinion, both of Chemnitius and Zanchy, that that exercise, which Christ honoured with his presence in his youth was a catechetical exercise. We that live in this age, have as much obligation as they, and God hath furnished to our hands the best help for it, that ever any age since Christ enjoyed. As chemists extract the spirits of herbs and minerals into some rare elixir, so have our venerable assembly (lately sitting at Westminster, now in glory) composed for us the most judicious and compendious system, that ever blessed this age. And to make it yet more useful, divers worthy hands have been employed, some in one method, some in another, to make those compendious answers more intelligible to the people. And yet I am of opinion, somewhat may be further done to advance that great design, in a third method, that shall not only make those points more intelligible, than in answering by yea and no: or drawing out the subservient answers to such a length, as too much charges the people's memory, but withal to intermix the most useful practical matter with what is doctrinal. If such a course might obtain in all our congregations, I think it would greatly discover our prudence, and turn richly to the account of our people's profit.

2. Meeting the needs of the sheep

Ministerial prudence discovers itself in the choice of such subjects as the needs of our peoples souls do most require, and call for. A prudent minister will study the souls of his people, more than the best human books in his library; and not choose what is easiest for him, but what is most necessary for them. Ministers that are acquainted with the state of their flocks, as they ought to be, will be seldom at a loss in the choice of the next subject: Their people's wants will choose their text, from time to time, for them. The greatest part of our congregations are poor, ignorant, and un-regenerated people that know neither their misery nor their remedy. This will direct us to the great doctrines of conviction, regeneration, and faith; and make us to sit with solicitous minds in our studies, pondering thus in our hearts: ' Lord, what course shall we take, and what words shall we choose, that may best convey the sense of their sin and danger, with the fulness and necessity of Christ, into their hearts.' Others are withering and decaying in their affections, or staggering and floating in their judgments: Prudence will enable the man of God to give to every one his proper food, or physic, in due season. This will make us spend more hours in our studies, and set to it with all our might and skill, that thereby we may both save ourselves, and them that hear us.

3. Clear and simple words

This ministerial wisdom will not only direct us thus in the choice of our subjects, but of the language too, in which we dress and deliver them to our people. It will tell you, a crucified stile best suits the preachers of a crucified Christ. A grave and proper stile becomes the lips of Christ's ambassadors. Prudence will neither allow us to be rude, nor affectedly flashy, in our expressions. Tertullian checks those preachers, whose sermons dress up Christianity in philosophical, rather than evangelical terms. Prudence will choose words that are solid, rather than florid: As a merchant will a ship by a sound bottom, and capacious hold, rather than a gilded head and stern. Words are but servants to matter. An iron key, fitted to the wards of the lock, is more useful than a golden one, that will not open the door to the treasure. Some of Christ's ministers excel in a neat and pleasing plainness of language. From this Austin was so affected with the style of Ambrose: ' With his sweet words, which I loved, came into my mind the duties which I neglected.' And Zanchy saith of Viret, 'I admired his eloquence, and the force it had in moving the affections.' Prudence will cast away a thousand fine words, for one that is apt to penetrate the conscience, and reach the heart. This made Basil look upon the famed allegories of his time, with a compassionate smile, saying, 'We take them for pretty witticisms, but things of little use or value in the ministry.' Who, in the last age, was ever honoured with more success in his ministry, than blessed Mr. Burroughs? And who ever excelled him in skill, to bring down the sublime mysteries of the gospel to the meanest capacity?

4. Preach affectionately

Ministerial prudence will shew us, of what great use our own affections are, for the moving of others ; and will therefore advise us, That, as ever we expect the truths we preach should operate the hearts of others, we first labour to work them in upon our own hearts. Such a preacher was St. Paul; he preached with tears accompanying his words, Phil. 3:18. An hot iron, though blunt, will pierce sooner than a cold one, though sharper. And why, my brethren, do we think, God hath commissioned us, rather than angels, to be his ambassadors? Was it not, among other reasons, for this? Because we having been under the same condemnation and misery ourselves, and felt both the terrors and consolations of the Spirit, (which angels experimentally know not), might thereby be enabled to treat with sinners more feelingly, and affectionately, in a way more accommodate to them, and therefore more apt to move and win them.

5. Treat ministry seriously

Ministerial prudence will direct the servants of Christ (who highly value, and earnestly long for the success of their labours) to be carefully the strictness and gravity of their deportment to maintain their esteem in the consciences of their people. In your pulpits, you are carrying on a treaty of peace betwixt God and them; and therefore it will not allow you to do anything out of your pulpits, to make the breach wider, or hinder the happy close between him and them. The fowler that spreads his net to take the birds, will not leave a feather, or make the least noise, to scare the bird he intends to take. Let not them who aim no higher than a bird, be more prudent and cautious, than you that are set to catch immortal souls. Remember that of Solomon, Prov. 11:30, ' He that winneth souls is wise.' Prudence will not allow the ministers of Christ to intermix themselves with vain company, and take the same liberty they do in vain jests, and idle stories. Nor will it allow, on the other side, a morose reservedness, and discouraging austerity; but temper gravity with condescending affability. To you that are juniors and candidates for the ministry, I will assume the boldness to address you with one seasonable word of advice; and it is this: Have a care of that light and airy spirit, which so much obtains everywhere in this unserious age. It was the charge of God against some ministers of old, that they were light persons, Rev. 3:4, and yet I cannot but think, comparatively speaking, with some of our times, they might pass for grave and serious. The people have eyes to see how we walk, as well as ears to hear what we say. It will be our wisdom and great advantage, to be able to say, as St. Paul did, Phil. 4:9, " The things which you have both heard and seen in me, do."

6. Prayerfulness

Ministerial prudence will send you often to your knees, to seek a blessing from God upon your studies and labours, as knowing all your ministerial success entirely depends thereupon, 1 Cor. 3:7. Those are the best sermons, that are obtained by prayer. Blessed Bradford studied upon his knees. Luther obtained more this way than by all his studies. If an honest husbandman could tell his neighbour, that the reason why his corn prospered better than his, was, because he steeped the seed in prayer, before he sowed it in the field; we may blush to think, how much more precious seed we have sown dry, and unsteeped in prayer, and by this neglect have frustrated our own expectation. Thus laying our foundations in the knowledge of principals choosing our subjects by the people's necessities; handling them in apt language; working them first upon your own affections, enforcing them by strict conversation, and steeping this holy seed in prayer; we shall approve ourselves the prudent ministers of Christ.

PRUDENCE WITH OTHERS

Having said thus much of prudence, with respect to our single personal concernment in the work of the ministry ; I come next to shew its great usefulness with respect to others, who are concerned either, 1. With us, as friendly assistants in our work. 2. Or against us, as enemies, who labour to obstruct and frustrate our work.

1. Gospel unity

As to our brethren and fellow-workers in the Lord, prudence will dictate and enjoin it upon us, that by the firmest union with them, we make their gifts and graces as useful as is possible, for the furtherance and advancement of our great and difficult work. We cannot be ignorant how much Satan hath gained, and Christ's interest hath sensibly lost, by those unhappy divisions and alienations amongst brethren, and fellow-labourers in the work of the Lord, Christ hath shed down variety of glorious ascension-gifts upon them, which are not capable of a full improvement, but in union and conjunction with each other. Gifts are improved in us by prayer and study, but the benefits of those gifts are shared among us by love and unity. Love and union bring every man's gifts and graces into the common bank, and instead of monopolies, they drive a free and open trade, to the great enriching of the church. There is not a greater, or more pleasant variety of qualities, smells, and colours, among the herbs and flowers with which the earth is variegated and decked, for the delight and service of men, than there is in the gifts and abilities of ministers, for the use and service of the church. One hath quickness of parts, but not so deep and solid a judgment: Another is grave and solid, but not so ready and presential. One is wary and reserved, another open and plain: One is melancholy and timorous, another cheerful and courageous. When these different gifts and qualities shine together in the church, heavens, what a glorious constellation do they make! And what sweet benign influences do they shed down upon the Lord's heritage! All these ministerial gifts and graces are improvable for Christ,

1. More privately, 2. More publicly, by brotherly union.

1. More privately. When God casts the lot of two, or more, fellow-labourers in the gospel, upon the same city, town, or neighbourhood; what a blessed advantage have they beyond solitary ministers, to carry on the work of the Lord cheerfully, vigorously, and successfully! Whilst love causes their hearts to clasp and close, how must their work be facilitated, sweetened, and prospered in their hands? But if once jars and jealousies get in amongst them; if pride, envy, or carnal interest dissolve the bond of brotherly love; if instead of planting for Christ, they once begin to supplant one another; no words are able to shew what a train of mischief and sins will now break in amongst them, to the great dishonour of Christ, and obstruction of the gospel. I do therefore in the name of Christ, as upon my bended knees, earnestly entreat and beseech my brethren, by all the regard they have to the honour of Christ, the souls of their people, their own comfort, or the success of their labours ; that no envying's, or strife's, no supplanting's, or detractions, be once admitted, or named among them.

Methinks it is scarce imaginable, that those who have so lately and severely smarted, should fall again into the same follies, for which God hath chastised them. 1. And as prudence directs us into the way of our profit and comfort, by this more private improvement of our gifts and graces, so into a more excellent way, by a general union and coalition with all our brethren, farther distant in place from us. It calls upon us to bury, and forget henceforth the factious names of distinction, growing out of our different apprehensions about smaller disciplinary points. How many fervent prayers have been poured out! How many excellent 'irenicums' have been written by those excellent ministers, that are now at perfect unity in heaven! Though they did not, yet I hope we and our children, shall reap the blessed fruits of those pious endeavours. God hath spoken with a strong hand to our pious and prudent brethren, in and about the great city of this kingdom: They have most wisely and seasonably projected this great and glorious design: They have followed it close with unwearied diligence, admirable patience. Christian humility and condescension; and, by the good hand of the Lord with them, have brought it at last to a comfortable issue. The happy result of their fervent prayers, and frequent brotherly consults, (all praise to the God of love and peace for it!) are now in our hands, in those blessed sheets, called Heads of agreement: Wherein God hath signally helped them to evidence their wisdom in the choice of words, and their humility and charity, in mutual and necessary concessions. They have, by the mouth of an eminent brother (whose praise is in the gospel, and whose hand hath eminently assisted in this service,) cheerfully offered up their praises to Jehovah-Shalom, for making the two sticks of Judah and Ephraim to become one stick in his own hand. And now, brethren, they wait, yea, give me leave to say, Christ waits as well as they, for our explicit consent, and cheerful suffrages. We have heard the joyful sound of our brethren's praises: Shall we not echo to it, and say, Hallelujah, and again Hallelujah? Ephraim shall no more envy Judah, nor Judah vex Ephraim: Our swords are turned into plowshares, and our spears into pruning hooks; The Lord hath this day rolled away our reproach. Thus prudence will direct us to carry it with love and unity towards our brethren, that labour in the work with us.

2. Dealing with enemies

Let us next see, what direction it gives us, with respect to our enemies who endeavour to obstruct and hinder the work of the Lord in our hands. If we be heartily engaged in the service of Christ, we must expect many adversaries, and strong oppositions; men that will raise clouds of reproaches, to darken our reputation among the people; men that will represent us to them as ignorant and unlearned, factious and seditious, erroneous and enthusiastical. Prudence, in this case, will restrain us from rendering reproach for reproach; and propound to us the best project in the world, for the vindication of our names, and success of our labours; and that is, that we so preach the gospel that the people may feel the power of Christ in our doctrine; and so live that they may see the beauty of Christ in our conversation; and so preaching and living, we shall bear down all the prejudices of the world before us. Such doctrine, seconded with such a conversation, like the sun in the heavens, will not only break up and scatter all clouds of reproach, but shed down their enlightening and enlivening influences upon the hearts of the people. I neither do, nor dare suggest and insinuate anything in this discourse, against any party or body of men; being convinced, that amongst those who differ from us, there are many learned, pious, and peaceable men, who can heartily rejoice to see the work of Christ carried on by those that follow not them. But some there are, almost in every place, who are more concerned for a ceremony, than for the substance of religion; for a tile upon the roof, than a stone in the foundation: Whose envy, if it cannot reach others by imitation, will be restless till it meet them by calumniation. In this case, ministerial prudence will carefully shun all occasions of exasperation; and if that care be not sufficient to avoid them, it will furnish us with that patience and constancy which will be sufficient to bear them. Thus we see the necessity and excellency of ministerial faithfulness and prudence, distinctly considered. Let us, next view them conjunctly in some special parts of our work, whereinto they shed down their joint and commixed influences. And these, among some others, are the duties of, 1. Defending truth against error. 2. Reproving offenders. 3. Dealing with distressed consciences.

(1). Defending the truth

There is great need of faithfulness and prudence, in defending the truths of Christ, against the errors of the times. Our faithfulness indeed will oblige us to do it; but prudence must direct us how to do it. The establishment of our people in the truth, is one special end of the institution of the ministry, Eph 4:11. But without the assistance of both these graces, that end is never like to be attained. A faithful minister dares not be silent, where the souls of his people are concerned; yet all his endeavours to secure them, will be to little purpose, if prudence be wanting in the management of that design. Prudence must both time our contentions, and regulate the manner of them. It will never suffer us to appear too soon, nor too late: Not too soon, because errors are sometimes best cured by neglect and in a little time grow weary of themselves; not too late, lest they get head, and be past retrieve: Hasty contenders, like young faulconers let fly the hawk with her hood on. Upon the other side, if friendship, or relation to seducers, stop our mouths too long, we may in a few days be entertained by them, (as Thyestes was by his brother Atreus) with the limbs of our own (spiritual) children. Prudence will not suffer our pulpits to ring with invectives against seducers, till the more private and gentle methods have been tried in vain; and then neither prudence nor faithfulness will admit of longer delay. But yet when they both advise us to engage, prudence must regulate the manner of the contention, and commands us to urge hard arguments with mild and soft language. Errorists are usually hot and passionate, proud and daring persons. Most true is that of Nazianzen, hot and haughty spirits are the causes of troubles and distractions in the church: Hot to hot will never do well. These heights and heats are best taken down, and cooled by strong and mild reasonings: "The wrath of man worketh not the righteousness of God.'

(2). Reproof

The joint commixed influences of both these graces, must be found in all our ministerial reproofs. Reprove we must, or we cannot be faithful; and prudently too, or we cannot be successful. He that is silent, cannot be innocent; and yet it is a measuring cast, whether cowardly silence be more prejudicial to the reprover, than indiscreet zeal may be to the reproved.

Faithfulness is loth to lose the soul of another for want of reproof: Prudence is jealous of losing it by the ill management of the reproof. Faithfulness saith, it is better to lose the smiles, than the souls of men: Prudence saith, to save both is best Reprehension is the chirurgery of the passions; and cutting-work is no easy or pleasant work. Sick and pained men are wayward, and pettish; but prudence will cast fetters upon their passions, and make them lie quiet, whilst faithfulness probes and searches their wounds to the bottom. Prudence can sometimes convey a reproof so effectually and inoffensively, that the conscience of the reproved shall sensibly feel it; and yet his passions not be awakened by the least injurious touch. Faithfulness considers, and urges the necessity of the duty; prudence considers the quality of the person, time, and manner of application. It will reach the sin, and yet (if possible) avoid the offence of the sinner. It sometime directs us to convict an offender, by transferring the offence by way of supposition to ourselves; sometimes by relating a suitable history, or folding down are- markable scripture threatening or example, as it were accidentally, to meet them. How prudently did Nathan prepare David, before he came to touch the quick, with, 'Thou art the man'? Above all, prudence adviseth us to keep ourselves pure from those sins we reprove in others; and when we must apply the precious oil of reproof to them, that we work it in with the warm, soft, gentle hand of love and compassion; and then the reproof is like to do good, and the reprover receive thanks for his kindness. 'Let the righteous smite me, it shall be a kindness: Let him reprove me, it shall be an excellent oil, which shall not break mine head," Psa. 141:5.

(3). Distressed consciences

Once more; their joint influences must also meet in all our dealings with distressed consciences. Conscience is a very tender thing, and when sick and distressed, needs to be handled both judiciously and tenderly. The wound must be searched, saith faithfulness; it must be searched skilfully, saith prudence: He that can so search and cure it, deserves that excellent encomium. One among a thousand Job 33:23. What expert and dexterous persons at this work, were our Greenham, Crook, Dod, Ball, and Borroughs! Every empiric can skin over a wound, but a faithful minister will search it thoroughly, and a prudent minister will heal it warily; Lest it fester at the bottom, and break out again with greater danger. It requires a great measure of both these graces, to bring general confused troubles to settle upon the right bottom; to direct a sin-sick soul to Christ, in the true gospel method; to furnish the tempted Christian with proper weapons against Satan's assaults, and teach him how to manage them; to dissolve the doubts, and remove the scruples which arise almost in every step of his way to Christ; and so to settle the fluctuating soul in a sweet and sure dependence upon him by faith. These things, I say, require much faithful prudence, and prudent faithfulness. And thus we see the manifold usefulness of both these graces in the servants and stewards of Christ. Of such I may say, as Christ in the text. Who then is faithful and wise servant. These servants (saith Piscator) are so rare, that out of a thousand scarce one man may be found that discharges that office aright. Christ hath not many such servants, yet, blessed be God, some such there are.

THE REWARD

And, 3. Whoever or wherever such faithful and wise servants are, Christ will abundantly reward them in the day of their account. Which casts me upon the third and last doctrinal head I promised to speak to. The glory prepared for, and promised to such servants of Christ, is elegantly laid out, in shining terms, by the prophet Daniel, Dan. 12:3. And they that be wise, shall shine as the brightness of the firmament; and they that turn many to righteousness, as the stars for ever and ever." A promise which points directly to wise and faithful ministers. What a beautiful sight is the azure canopy of heaven, when it is about to shut its beautiful eyelids in the serene evening! And much more when it is about to open them with a smile or blush, in the dawning of the ruddy morning! And how is that beauty again outvied by the glory of the stars where the pleasing lights spark and twinkles! How doth one star excel another in glory ! Yet thus, and more than thus; even above the brightness of the sun itself shall the servants of Christ shine; who by their faithfulness and prudence, have instrumentally turned many into righteousness! The question about degrees of glory in heaven is not necessary, but problematical. We reject with abhorrence the popish doctrine of diversity of glories, as founded in the diversity of merits: Nor is it questioned, among the orthodox, whether there be an equality of glory, as to the essentials; but only in respect to the accidentals, and concomitants: Amongst which, they place the additional glory and joy of such ministers, whose faithful and prudent labours God hath blessed, and crowned with the conversion and edification of many souls. And of this the apostle speaks, 1 Thess. 2:19, 20. "For what is our hope, or joy, or crown of rejoicing? Are not even ye, in the presence of our Lord Jesus Christ at his coming? For ye are our glory and joy." Where we find a very remarkable gradation. He calls his Thessalonian converts, his hope, his joy, nay, his crown of rejoicing.' His hope, that is, the matter of his hope, that they should be saved, His joy, as they had already given him abundant cause of joy, in their conversion to Christ by his ministry. And the "crown of his rejoicing in the presence of Christ, at his coming- This is an high strain indeed. The meaning, I suppose, is that the fruit and success of his ministry among them, would add to his crown, and redound to his glory in the day of Christ. 'O brethren ! who would not study and pray, spend and be spent, in the service of such a bountiful Master! Is it not worth all our labours and sufferings, to come with all those souls we instrumentally bring to Christ: and all that we edified, reduced, confirmed, and comforted in the way to heaven ; and say, Lord, here am I, and the children thou hast given me? To hear one spiritual child say. Lord, this is the minister, by whom I believed: Another, this is he, by whom I was edified, established, and comforted. This is the man that resolved my doubts, quickened my dying affections, reduced my soul, when wandering from the truth. O blessed be thy name, that I ever saw his face, and heard his voice! What think we of this, brethren? But far beyond this; what will it be to hear Christ, the prince of pastors, say in that day, "Well done good and faithful servant; thou hast been faithful over a few things, I will make thee ruler over many things: enter thou into the joy of thy Lord," Mat, 25:21 . O sirs we serve a good Master, who is not unrighteous to forget our work and labour of love for his name-sake. He keeps an exact account of all your fervent prayers, of all your instructive and persuasive sermons; and all your sighs, groans, and panting's, with every tear and drop of sweat, are placed like marginal notes against your labours in his book, in order to a full reward. But 1 have far out-run my own intention, and (I doubt) your patience too, in the doctrinal part.

APPLICATION

I consider to whom I speak, and shall be the shorter in the application; which I shall dispatch apace, in three uses.

1. For Information,

2. For Reprehension.

3. For Exhortation.

Use I

And first for our information, briefly, in two or three consectaries. Consectary 1. By this it appears, Christ hath established an order and government in his house, which none must violate. The church is a well ordered family, or household, whereof Christ is the Head, Christians members, ministers stewards, the ordinances food to be dispensed by them in season. Every one is to keep his own place and station. Pastors must faithfully feed and govern the flocks of Christ, Acts 20:28. People must know, honour, and obey those that are over them in the Lord, 1 Thess. 5:12. Heb. 13:17. The one must not impose, nor the other usurp! but each walk according to the rule of Christ, with a right foot, ordinately and comely. This order is the church's beauty, Col. 2:5. and truly we may expect so much of Christ's presence, as we have of his rule and order amongst us, and no more. O that the rules and orders of his house were better known, and observed! then ministers and people would clearly understand, what they are to expect from each other in the way of duty, and each person keep his proper station. Ministers would not invade the civil callings of the people, nor the people the sacred calling of the ministry; but all things would move ordinately. The pleasure of such a sight, would as much transport gracious souls with joy and pleasure, as the order of Solomon's house did the queen of the South. Consectary 2. In the light of this truth, we may also read our duty, how we ought to govern ourselves in the ordination of men to the ministerial office. This office is to be committed unto faithful and able men, 2 Tim. 2:2. not to novices, 1 Tim. 3:6. I know the necessities of the churches are great, but no more haste (I beseech you) to supply their wants, than good speed. That is soon enough, that is well enough. It is a less hazard, to put an ignorant rustic into an apothecary's shop, to compound and prepare medicines for men's bodies, than to trust a man, destitute both of faithfulness and prudence, with the dispensation of Christ's ordinances to men's souls. Some men are moved by pitiful low ends. 1 Sam. 2:36. " Put me into the priest's office, that I may eat a piece of bread." Some by ambition, conceiting themselves as able and holy as the best Numb. 16:3. What men's secret ends are, we cannot know ; but their qualifications for that work we may, and ought to know. We are solemnly charged, to ' lay hands suddenly upon no man,' 1 Tim. 5:22. In Solomon's time, the Jews were exceeding careful and wary in admitting proselytes, because they were then a flourishing and prosperous state; not adulterous in time of adversity, as Josephus observes. I would discourage none that appear to have pious inclinations, matched with competent qualifications. Many be useful, that cannot be excellent. Weaker gifts, rooted in a gracious heart, will grow by using; but nothing grows without a root. I think the plainest men have done the greatest service in the church of Christ as tender-eyed Leah brought forth more children than beautiful Rachel. But still fidelity and prudence are indispensable qualifications. Consectary 3. If there be such rewards, in the hand of Christ, for all his faithful and wise servants; Then we have no just cause or reason to repent of our choice of this office, whatever sufferings and reproaches it hath or yet may expose us to. I believe none of us ever yet felt such straits, endured such miseries, or sustained such labours, as the apostle mentions to have befallen him, 2 Cor. 11:23, 24, 25, 26, 27. and yet he heartily thanks the Lord Jesus Christ, (for all that) who had counted him faithful, and put him into the ministry. Brethren, we have served a good Master, and have cause to admire his care over us, and bounty to us; and whatever we have suffered, we may say to them that shall succeed us, as Tossanus did to his children and kindred, in his last will and testament : ' I charge you my dear children and relations, That ye never be ashamed of the evangelical truth, either for the sake of offences arising from "within the church, or of persecutions from without it. Truth may labour, but cannot be suppressed: And I have often found by experience, the Lord to be wonderfully present with them, that walk before him diligently and uprightly.' O he hath been a good God to us ! he hath covered us in days of danger, made provision for us and ours, and yet his best rewards are behind. Let none scare at the reproaches and persecutions that attend the gospel.

Use II

This point casts an ireful countenance upon all unfaithful and imprudent ministers, who give their people the chaff for the wheat, and stones for bread; who glory in the title, and live upon the profits, but neither feed the flock, nor mind the account. They preach, they play, because they must do so; but none are the better for their prayers, or preaching. They seem to labour an hour or two in a week, but their labours turn to no account; nor can he expected to turn to any good account, whilst they are neither animated by faithfulness, nor guided by prudence. Agricola, writing de anvnant'thus subterraneis, tells us of a certain kind of spirits that converse with minerals, and much infest those that work in them. They seem to busy themselves according to the custom of workmen; they will dig and cleanse, melt and sever the metals, yet when they are gone, the workmen do not find that there is anything done. I came not hither (I confess) to deal with this sort of men; and therefore shall leave them to consider the words immediately following my text, which, like a thunder-clap from the mouth of Christ, discharges woes and threatening's upon them; vs. 48 to the end : " If that evil servant shall say in his heart, My Lord delayeth his comin ; and shall begin to smite his fellow-servants, and to eat and drink with the drunken: The Lord of that servant shall come in a day that he looketh not for him, and in an hour that he is not aware of; and shall cut him asunder, and appoint him his portion with hypocrites. There shall be weeping, and gnashing of teeth." Who can aggravate their misery more, than these words of Christ have done? But I am principally concerned at this time about our own defects, both in faithfulness, and in prudence; though neither of these (I hope) to be totally wanting in us, yet our defects and short-comings may, and must greatly humble us. Our vain expense of much precious time, our shuffling haste in so weighty a study as the salvation of our people is; our sinful silence, when conscience saith, reprove; our coldness and dead-heartedness; our unserious and unprofitable converses; our pride and ostentation of gifts; our neglect and personal conferences: all these evidently discover, that both our brains and bowels need more strength and tenderness. I will not insist here upon these particulars, (let us do that in our studies) but hasten to the exhortation, and therein to the close of this discourse.

Use III

Are faithfulness and prudence the essential requisites of the servants and stewards of Christ's house? And will he so amply reward them in whomsoever he finds them? Then let it be our care and study to approve ourselves to him, such as he here describes and encourages. But who am I, to manage such a work as this, among men every way above me! However, you have called me to this service, and Christ hath directed me to this subject: And should I now silently pass over this part of my work, how shall I approve myself, either a faithful, or a wise servant to him that sent me." I despair of ever having such another opportunity; I see many faces in this assembly, whom I shall never see any more in this world. I speak to the ministers of Christ, the guides and pastors of so many flocks. May I be in the least instrumental to quicken them in their duties, their respective numerous congregations will reap the benefit of it. My brethren, this is the day I have often wished for, when in the sad and silent years that are past, I have been searching my own heart, and enquiring into the causes of God's indignation (as I doubt not you also have done;) I have bewailed the aforementioned defects before the Lord, and engaged my soul by solemn promise to him, that if he would once more open the door of liberty, I would (through his grace) labour to reform, and do my utmost to persuade all my brethren to exercise more ministerial faithfulness and prudence. And now I am where my soul hath long desired to be, and the vows of God are upon me; suffer therefore (dear brethren) yea, suffer from unworthy me, This word of exhortation: Take heed to your ministry that you fulfil it: Take heed to yourselves and to the flocks over which the Holy Ghost hath made you overseers. Let us so study and preach, let us so pray and converse among our people, that we may both save ourselves, and them that hear us; let us frugally and industriously husband our time and talents for Christ; let us prudently contrive, zealously and unanimously execute our holy contrivances, for the advancement of his kingdom and interest in the world: These are plotting times, wicked men are everywhere plotting to disturb the civil peace; let us have our plot too, an honest plot, how to advance the interest of Christ in the souls of our people; wherein we shall also promote and secure the civil peace of that happy government we live under. Let us learn prudence from our past follies, and constancy from our past experiences. I look upon you that are aged ministers, as seasoned timber, that hath lain out near thirty years in the weather, yet neither warped, rained, nor rotten, I confess, in all this time, the sun hath not much tried the force of his influence upon us, though the storms have. I suspect our greatest danger will be in the sunshine of liberty. If we hold it now, and manage this trial by liberty, with eminent faithfulness and prudence, humility and peaceableness, zeal and diligence; Christ may account us fit materials to build his house. Let us now redeem our many silent Sabbaths, by double and triple improvements of those we enjoy: Let none of us dare to bring our old sins into our new pulpits. Then will the Prince of pastors delight in us here, and crown our prudent faithfulness with a full reward hereafter. In order whereunto, give me leave to hint (for I can do no more than hint) these three things by way of motive, which are worth thinking on: We have a solemn charge given us by Christ. We have a solemn account to pass shortly with

Christ. We have now a great opportunity to improve for Christ.

1. We have a solemn charge given us by Christ 2 Tim. 4:1, 2. " I charge thee therefore before God, and the Lord Jesus Christ, who shall judge the quick and the dead at his appearing, and his kingdom ; preach the word, be instant in season, and out of season ; reprove, rebuke, exhort with all long-suffering and doctrine." It must be a powerful opiate indeed, that can so benumb and stupefy the conscience of a minister, as that he shall not feel the awful authority of such a charge. The precious and immortal souls of men are committed to us; souls, about which God hath concerned his thoughts from eternity; for the purchase of which Christ hath shed his own blood; for the winning and espousing of which to himself, he hath put you into this office; at whose hands he will also require an account of them in the great day.

2. We have a solemn account at that day to pass "with Christ. Heb. 13:17, 'We watch for their souls, as those that must give account." And what can more powerfully excite to faithful diligence

in the discharge of duty, than the consideration of that day ! Which the apostle had mentioned, in 2 Cor. 5:10. this awful appearance before the judgment-seat of Christ; he immediately infers, verse 11. 'Knowing therefore the terror of the Lord, we persuade men.' O brethren ! let us beware of committing, or of neglecting anything, that may bring us within the compass of the terrors of that day. Let our painfulness and faithfulness, our constancy and seriousness, compel a testimony from our congregations, as the apostle did from his. Acts 28:26. "That we are pure from the blood of all men."

3. We have a great opportunity to improve for Christ; which if we do, we shall fulfil his charge, and escape the terrors of his judgment in that great day. We have now (if I mistake not) the fairest season we ever enjoyed since we first preached Christ; if this be lost, I question whether we may ever expect the like. There is great odds betwixt our present circumstances at our return to our flocks, and our past circumstances when we left them, and that both upon our own account, and upon theirs. 1. Upon our own account: We were then young, and (comparatively) unexperienced ministers to

what we are now. Though we have too many defects and weaknesses still to lament, yet I am persuaded we have not spent so many years among trials, fears, and sufferings in vain. These things, I am persuaded, have greatly improved our acquaintance with God, and our own hearts. It will be as sad as strange, if they have not. God hath been training us up in faith, humility, patience, and self-denial in this school of affliction. When we could not preach the doctrine of faith, we were reduced, by a blessed necessity, to live the life of faith. The rules of patience, humility, and satisfaction in the will of God, we were wont to prescribe from our pulpits to the people, we were necessitated to practise and apply to ourselves in our sad solitudes, and various distresses, through which the Lord hath led us. So that now we come better furnished to the work, than ever before. And I hope I have ground for you, brethren, to say, as the apostle, of his coming to the Romans, that you come among them " in the fulness of the blessing of the gospel of Christ." 3. There is great odds upon the people's account: Many of them were full-fed, and wanton, when we left them; they are hungry, and sharp set, at our return to them. An hungry appetite appears in the people in many places, not without great cause and reason. They are willing to take any pains: your words now drop upon them as the clouds upon the clefted earth. O what an opportunity doth this give to accomplish the great ends of our ministry among them? Lift up your eyes, and behold the fields, are they not even white unto the harvest ? Let husbandmen rather lose their seed-time and harvest, than we lose so precious a season, so great, so rich an opportunity as this. I have finished what concerns you, my reverend and dear brethren, and fellow-labourers in the Lord's harvest: A word or two remains to be spoken to the people, and I have done. You have heard what a variety of duty lies upon us, and what difficulty in every part thereof; yet all our labours would be light, and our pains pleasant, might we see more fruits, and success of them amongst you. Your barrenness and unpersuadableness, your divisions and instability cost us more, than all our other pains in our studies and pulpits. How easily and sweetly would the plough go, would you but set both your hands of prayer and obedience to assist us in that work. You have now as blessed an opportunity as your souls can desire, yea, that very season of mercy some of you have a long time anxiously desired. You have confessed to God, that you once sinned us out of our pulpits; God forbid you should next sin us into our graves. If you be wanton children at a full table, our enemies are not so far off, but God can quickly call them in to cure your wantonness, by taking away the cloth. The stewards of Christ provide choice dishes for you, even feasts of fat things full of marrow; and serve it into your souls upon the knee of prayer in due season: have a care of despising it, if at any time the dishes be not garnished as you expect, with curious figures, and flowers of rhetoric. The Lord give you hungry appetites, sound digestions, and thriving souls; then shall ye be our crown of rejoicing, and we yours in the day of our Lord Jesus Christ: To the word of whose grace I commend you all, which is able to build you up, and give you an inheritance among them that are sanctified.

Printed in Great Britain
by Amazon